UP AGAINST IT

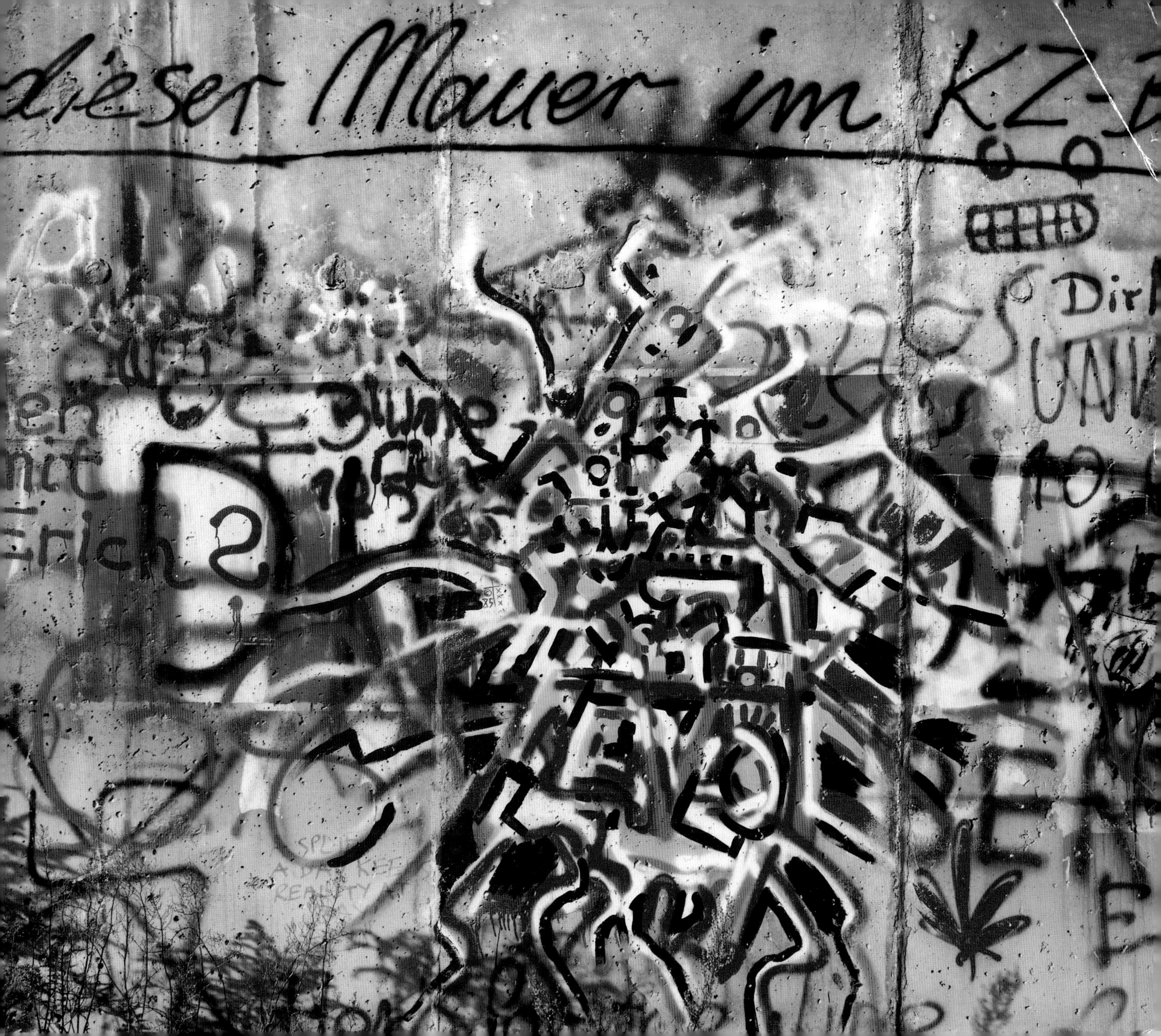
dieser Mauer im KZ-
Blume
Erich
Dirk
UNV

# UP AGAINST IT

## PHOTOGRAPHS OF THE BERLIN WALL

### LELAND RICE

ESSAY BY CHARLES E. McCLELLAND    FOREWORD BY VAN DEREN COKE
UNIVERSITY OF NEW MEXICO PRESS    ALBUQUERQUE

Library of Congress Cataloging in Publication Data

Rice, Leland, 1940–

Up Against It: Photographs of the Berlin Wall/Leland Rice: essay by
Charles E. McClelland; foreword by Van Deren Coke.—1st ed.

p. cm.

ISBN 0-8263-1291-8

1. Berlin wall (1961– )  2. Graffiti—Germany—Berlin.
3. Street art—Germany—Berlin  I. McClelland, Charles E., 1940–  . II. Title.

DD881.R49  1991          91-295
943.1′55—dc20            CIP

Photographs on preceding pages:
*Ost, West Zu Hause Best* (diptych), 1985
(frontispiece) *Untitled* (colored arrows), 1987

# CONTENTS

# FOREWORD

I FIRST MET LELAND RICE IN 1962 WHEN HE ENROLLED IN A photography course I was teaching at Arizona State University. He was a business major but soon found that making photographs gave him a creative outlet and a feeling of satisfaction, a feeling that has never waned. After graduate work at San Francisco State University, he became an active teacher of creative photography at various schools and universities in southern California. He used his considerable knowledge of the history of photography as a means of developing in his students an awareness of the traditions of the medium. In order to expand his own aesthetic framework, he studied contemporary painting and became friends with a number of avant-garde artists in the Los Angeles area. Their aesthetic concerns were of great interest to him and he sought to parallel in photography some of the achievement of a sculptor like Larry Bell and the environmental artist James Turrell.

In the mid-1970s Rice produced black-and-white pictures of vacant interiors that collectively were given the title *Wall Sites.* Although no people appear in these pictures, a human presence is strongly implied, creating a sense of mystery like one might experience when viewing surreal paintings. In the late 1970s and into the 1980s, Rice took as his subject walls of painters' studios where paint had splashed beyond the edges of a painting as it was being applied to the canvas. What Rice was doing was photographing in color the rectangular shapes left on a wall after the paintings had been removed. The splashed paint speaks of action by the artist whose work was removed from the room and, in a way, alludes to Rice's early *Wall Site* pictures. By choosing to photograph the color around the vacant space left on the walls, he tied his pictures to the concerns of Minimalism and Color Field painting as represented in the work of artists ranging from Jules Olitski to Brice Marden. The sense of mystery courted in his early work was still a factor in these photographs, but the turn to color added another intriguing element. From a formal standpoint it deepened the spatial illusion and created a lyrical, poetic atmosphere that possesses a feeling of

expansiveness like one experiences when viewing a Richard Die-
benkorn *Ocean Park* painting.

From these intellectual pictures Rice turned to photographing
imagery on the West German side of the Berlin Wall. He began this
work in 1983 and has visited Berlin numerous times in the last
eight years to become better acquainted with the graffiti marking
the Wall, from which were extracted certain elements that he found
especially meaningful. Rice, who refers to himself as a "visual ar-
chaelogist," extracted visual fragments from the Wall by focusing
close-up on aspects of brightly colored pictographic art, symbols,
poetry, slogans, and familiar expletives that covered its surface in
layers. The imagery is laden with social, political, and cultural
history, which he perceptively blended with formal concerns sim-
ilar to those of his earlier soft-hued color prints of artists' studio
walls. Remarking on his Berlin Wall series, Rice has said, "I wanted
to get closer to something that would deal with human life—something that would be more engaging and penetrate what's on our
minds. Without disengaging myself from my formal background I
wanted something deeper."

*(overleaf) Der Super 8, 1983*

In the mélange of pictures on the Wall, simple earthly utterances vied for attention with ideological posturing. A great variety of vernacular styles interspersed with sophisticated visual language was used to address the tensions that existed between East and West Berlin, a tragic disunity that symbolized global conflict until the extraordinary events of late 1989. The emotional intensity of some statements carry them beyond any barrier of language, while other passages are directed to people who have special knowledge. This means the uninitiated remain largely ignorant of their layered meaning, but even in such cases the intent can be felt, if not completely decoded. Often these are the images that stick in one's consciousness. With great ingenuity Rice adjusted his lens to record the collective message of these marks on the ugly Wall that was continuously watched by armed guards on the East German side. The Wall is largely gone, but his pictures remain, which is important for they evoke the spirit of the place which in turn reflects the spirit of our time with all of its conflicts and anxieties.

Van Deren Coke
*Professor Emeritus, University of New Mexico*

"For the stone will cry out of the wall."

Habakkuk 2:11

a

# THE BERLIN WALL
## From Cold War Symbol to Cultural Artifact

ON NOVEMBER 9, 1989, THE BERLIN WALL CEASED TO EXIST. AS THE world watched through the eye of television, thousands of Berliners, east and west, danced and lounged atop the gray concrete cadaver. While the mute corpse still lay there, Berliners, champagne bottles in hand, drank and sang of its demise in a happy wake for the oppression, division, and injustice it had symbolized. The Wall had ceased to exist, not yet as a physical relic, but already as a symbol.

Without the will and capacity of the Stalinist regime of East Germany to support that symbol, which it had erected and given life to, the Wall became merely *a* wall. Once it ceased to mean political control of millions (and struggle against that control); ceased to mean the division of Germany, Europe, and the world into hostile camps; ceased to threaten death or imprisonment for all who approached one of its sides—then the power of its chilling concrete mass vanished. Official crews punched holes in its remains

cease - aufhören
exist - existieren
lounge - sich rekeln
concrete - das Beton
der Körper
demise - das Ableben
capacity - der Inhalt
support - die Stütze

Figure a. *West Berlin viewing platform near Martin-Gropius-Bau, 1984.*

to let inhabitants of the two parts of divided Berlin visit each other freely. Even faster, tourists and souvenir-hunters (*Mauerspechte* or "Wall woodpeckers") chipped and chiseled, reducing long segments to pathetic skeletons of twisted rebar with tufts of crumbling cement clinging to them.

The Berlin Wall was thus always a symbol, or rather a set of symbols. It was not only much more than the 164 kilometers (about 100 miles) of reinforced-concrete slabs, neatly raked no-man's land, barbed wire, secondary walls, tank (and car) traps, watchtowers, and frequent patrols by heavily armed *Vopos* ("People's Police") and vicious *Mauerhunde* ("Wall dogs"). All this was, in a way, merely concretization of symbols. For the Stalinists who built it, it symbolized the coercion and control—naturally for a "higher goal"—essential for the continuation of their regime, to give them time to "build real existing socialism" that would eventually make the Wall unnecessary. For West Berliners, it symbolized many different and complex things, but hardly that. The Wall called on the traditional resilience of Berliners, on their wit and inventiveness. And for the western face of the Wall, they invented a new kind of cultural symbolism. What began as graffiti on a desolate, bare public surface bloomed into a unique expression of a very special culture—Berlin Wall art. The French novelist and culture minister André Malraux had prophesied decades before the idea of a "museum without walls," the coming entry of art into everyday life. West Berliners (and not a few artists from elsewhere) managed to make their Wall into an outdoor art display connected to everyday life. In this way, over many miles of its surface, the Wall became a sort of museum exhibiting art that mostly mocked it, foretold its demise, or subverted its purpose for the glories of unregulated human self-expression.

In a society that strikes many foreigners as highly regulated and almost obsessively law-abiding, the Wall occupied a unique zone of ambiguity. The structure itself was erected on the territory of East Germany. Even the patrols of People's Police could not be trusted near their own side of the Wall (many found ways of "jumping" it), let alone to patrol the western face. West Berlin authorities were also prohibited from regulating matters having to do with the western face. Thus the western-facing side of the Wall was literally and figuratively a "gray area," a virtual challenge to urban graffitists. Especially in the more densely populated districts near the old center of Berlin, such as Kreuzberg and Wedding, graffiti gradually had to share space with a wild profusion of murals by the 1980s. Apparently because of the lack of authority over the west side of the Wall, the city fathers of West Berlin did not undertake any systematic cataloging or photographing of these changing miles of murals and were equally powerless to prevent the souvenir-hunters from demolishing most of this Wall art in the months after November 1989. Except for a few sections saved by the East German authorities (and presumably destined for a future museum exhibit), Wall art has disappeared forever.

Fortunately Leland Rice has been photographing this Wall for many years. The collection in this book constitutes works of art in themselves, and they can and should be enjoyed without commentary. The photographs are in the main not intended to document or catalogue Wall art, either, but to use it as a point of departure for the photographing artist's imagination in choice, composition, color, and line. Yet they also convey a good idea of what Wall art was like.

It is not the purpose of this introduction to discuss the artist's photographs, but rather to provide for them a historical framework.

What political forces led to the building and demolition of the Wall? What did it symbolize? What kind of special urban culture produced the largely anonymous murals and graffiti?

## WHY THE WALL?

When the "big three" Allies against Nazi Germany (Britain, the United States, and the Soviet Union), later joined by France, decided to occupy the defeated country and its capital, they anticipated a harmonious cooperation in peacetime. Otherwise, the stationing of Allied troops in four sectors of Berlin, surrounded by a Russian-occupied zone, with access to supply lines only at the forebearance of the Russians, would have made little sense.

The Cold War, however, quickly turned Allied harmony into confrontation, and nowhere was this face-off more tense than in Germany and Berlin. The three Western Allies pursued their own policies in their occupation zones, leading to the currency reform of 1948 and the foundation of the Federal Republic in 1949. The Berlin blockade by the Russians (1948–49) was one response; when this failed owing to the successful Allied "airlift" to supply the city, the establishment of the German Democratic Republic was another. The GDR was allowed by the Russians to install itself in East Berlin, because Berlin was recognized as the legal capital of a future *united* Germany. The Allies did not promote the location of the capital of the Federal Republic (FRG) in West Berlin, however. The status of West Berlin was still under Allied sovereignty, long after most sovereign rights over West Germany had been returned to Bonn. But there were clear and strong ties between West Berlin and West Germany, including heavy financial subsidies of the former by the latter. It is useful to bear this "special relationship" in mind, for it explains many of the anomalies of West Berlin life from the 1940s until October 1990.

Another peculiarity of the division and occupation of Germany was that practice (division into two German states) and theory (the eventual restoration of a united and sovereign, if territorially somewhat smaller, Germany) yawned ever wider apart with the passage of the decades. The integration of the FRG and the GDR into the respective multinational pacts, politico-economic (European Community/COMECON) and military (NATO/Warsaw Pact), seemed to

Figure b. *Checkpoint Charlie, Allied border crossing, 1985.*

b

bolster the permanence of national division. Churchill's metaphor of an Iron Curtain dividing Europe took on the reality of a barbed wire curtain along the frontiers between the two Germanies.

Everywhere, that is, except in Berlin, where the citizens could still come and go across the sectoral boundaries. East Berliners could and did step through the Brandenburg Gate to get back and forth to jobs in West Berlin (and vice versa). Thanks to the Allies' maintenance of their air access from the FRG to West Berlin, East Germans needed only walk through that gate and board a plane to go to West Germany. Under the law of the Federal Republic, they were considered citizens automatically, entitled to support and a new life. The GDR could and did make it hard, then all but impossible, for its citizens to cross the western border to a new life in the FRG; but it could hardly keep its own citizens out of its own capital, East Berlin, or stop them (under the joint-occupation rules of the Big Four) from passing freely to the western sectors of the city.

Many did so. As the gap in the standards of living and personal freedom between the FRG and the GDR continued to widen, millions of East Germans "voted with their feet" and left. Unlike citizens of the other Soviet-bloc countries, East Germans could choose easily to join the Western side in the Cold War without serious legal problems or changing their language. In the booming economy of the West German *Wirtschaftswunder* (economic miracle), skilled labor was in great demand. The GDR was being bled dry of its better workers and professionals, without whom no society—let alone an increasingly Stalinist one—could hope to build a shining model of socialism able to compete with the West.

The regime of Walter Ulbricht, which had beaten back a workers' uprising in 1953 with the aid of Soviet tanks, concluded by 1961 that this hemorrhage had to be stanched. The government of Nikita Khruschchev in Moscow, mindful of the dangers of confronting the Western Allies, but also gambling that they would not go to war, finally agreed. The GDR put up barbed-wire blockades between the eastern and western sectors of Berlin on August 13, 1961. Conditioned by years of Soviet threats about taking over all of West Berlin, the Allies were apparently both caught off guard and perhaps also relieved that the Soviet gambit, when it came, fell short of their worst fears. After October 1961, when Soviet and American tanks faced off at the Wall for the only time during the Cold War, the Allies eventually concluded that Russia would not invade West Berlin but did nothing physically to tear down the barricades. They stoutly defended their right to remain in West Berlin, but to prevent a world nuclear war, they shied away from a military showdown over the Wall.

The East Germans, loudly proclaiming their peaceful intentions and their alleged desire to keep out spies, began replacing the barbed-wire with the now-familiar permanent "Wall of Peace," to cite their jargon. The willingness of the ruling SED (Socialist Unity Party) to shoot and kill its citizens who tried to penetrate the Wall, and to mete out harsh prison sentences to those that even attempted "Flight of the Republic" soon enough slowed the river of defectors to a steady, if dramatic trickle. For the hundreds who tunneled, swam, flew, or were smuggled in vehicles under, over, or around the Wall, some 200 were killed trying to breach it, and thousands of others were caught and sent to jail.

Yet, despite the bitter denunciations of the "Wall of Shame" in West Berlin and the Federal Republic, despite ritual trips to the Wall by Allied leaders beginning with John F. Kennedy, this inhumane structure did for the GDR what it had hoped. Combined with strict controls on traveling by GDR citizens (incidentally re-inforced by the other Soviet-block countries' authorities), the GDR managed to lock its population into a workhouse where the only serious alternative was to try to "build socialism." For a time, the GDR had a breathing spell to build up its economy to a point where it was the envy of the Soviet bloc (if still not of the West). By dangling the bait of more humane conditions for the workhouse inhabitants, the regime was even able to wangle concessions from the detente-minded governments of the FRG beginning in the late 1960s. For such concessions as allowing old-age pensioners to travel to the West, the GDR received what it avidly craved—some steps toward its own recognition as a country, financial credits, and other assurances of its continued existence. It even "sold" its prisoners "guilty" of "Attempted Flight of the Republic" to the FRG for hard currency.

The Wall remained because it worked for the GDR—long after it celebrated itself as a viable, internationally recognized state with a relatively strong economy and the achievement of "real existing socialism." No matter how confident the regime had become, it could not dispense with the Wall and the ban on the human right of free movement that it symbolized. Only months before he was swept from power, the SED leader Erich Honecker cockily stated that he could not foresee the end of the Wall. In so doing, he tacitly acknowledged that it was the symbolic bedrock (not just cinderblock) on which the GDR was built.

The consequences of the Wall for Berliners were less happy. The separation of family members in what had been until 1961 a single city was one example of hardship. The director of the psychiatric division of the largest East Berlin hospital, Dietfried Müller-Hegemann, up to then a convinced Communist, began to notice (and secretly record) the incidence of psychiatric disorders among his patients separated from their loved ones by the Wall. As a caring physician, he was unable to persuade the authorities to apply the obvious cure—letting the patients go. He finally went himself, and published his findings in a book entitled *Die Mauerkrankheit* ("The Wall Sickness") in 1973. His own escape, with his wife, was marked by the type of elaborate plotting and heart-wrenching family decisions that characterized many escapes from behind the Wall (his grown children, at their insistence, had to remain behind as "pawns" to let their parents leave the country on legitimate, but separate

Figure c. *Transitory graffiti at walled street, 1985.*

c

scientific and medical-treatment trips). Müller-Hegemann's book is but one of many that detail the agony and emotional deterioration of otherwise "sane" people on both sides of the Wall. Only those finally adjudged clinically insane, who kept breaking out of asylums and "leaping" back and forth across the Wall, as documented in Peter Schneider's sensational novel *Der Mauerspringer* (*The Wall Jumper*) were immune to its emotional impact.

The effects on West Berliners were no less serious. Cut off not only from friends and relatives in the East, West Berliners long suffered a double emotional bind. Eventually the expanding "human alleviations" worked out between the GDR and the FRG meant that West Germans could visit East German more easily; but until only very recently, West Berliners were not included in most of these "alleviations." Nor could they travel into the surrounding hinterland, a fact producing a certain feeling of claustrophobia that could not be relieved by traveling to West Germany, the rest of Europe, or any place in the world but their own backyard.

Anybody who has visited Berlin in the last few years may have observed what I did on several occasions, standing on the platforms overlooking the Wall on the western side. The successive layers of main Wall (over which one peered), no-man's land with mines, carefully raked desert soil to detect footprints, path for double Vopo patrols with dogs, and inner and lower wall, gave the impression of a regime ready to sacrifice hundreds of square miles of inner-city real-estate for its symbolic determination to crush the spirit of its inhabitants. Most older citizens (the first Wall generation) had long since caved in and gone about their daily business. But a Vopo patrol would go by and turn a corner. Suddenly a young man, up to then indolently sunning himself on a balcony in East Berlin, would stand up, unfurl a West German flag on the balcony rail, and wave. Just long enough to anticipate the next Vopo patrol, wave a final time, roll up the flag, and go back to sunbathing. These were the people, I supposed, who caused near-riot conditions in East Berlin when Western rock groups would give open-air concerts on the western side of the Wall in full amplified earshot of down-town East Berlin. These were the young people who began going to Peace Group (*Friedensbewegung*) discussions in the previously moribund churches of East Germany, despite police harassment.

That waving rebel was not, I think, trying to endorse the "Western way of life," capitalism, or "West German revanchism," although those are things he would have been tried for in the GDR, if caught. He captured the all-but-universal resentment of the Wall and its restrictions on freedom of movement among the whole GDR population. As an American scholar "privileged" to travel in East Germany and East Berlin for a quarter-century, and after many conversations with people ranging from party members in elegant apartments to anonymous workers in grimy bars, I heard only one unanimous complaint: "they" ought to let us travel. Even the most convinced believer in the goals of the regime, from factory worker to privileged member of the Leipzig *Gewandhaus* Orchestra, claimed their loyalty to the regime was undermined by the *Reiseverbot*— the ban on travel. The Wall was the symbol of that. It would not be too much of an exaggeration to say that the Wall, designed to save the GDR as a state and the SED as its ruling party, in fact bred the universal revulsion that brought all of them down.

But that is the East German side of the Wall. Wall art is a story of West Berlin, and to that we must now turn.

## WEST BERLIN
### *Peculiarities of a Cold-War Front-Line City*

Berlin has seen many changes in its 750-year history, growing from a collection of fishing villages to the chief bureaucrat-and-garrison town of the ambitious Kingdom of Prussia, to the capital of united Germany in 1871 and a major industrial metropolis by the beginning of the twentieth century. By no means the cradle of Nazism, "Red Berlin" retained a tradition as a center of left-wing political activity. But as the Nazi capital, the city suffered the consequences, including devastation by bombs, artillery, and postwar looting and dismantling of industrial assets.

The breakdown of Allied unity after the war was particularly sharp in Berlin, where the smooth functioning of the city's recovery was impaired. The Soviets had the advantage of surrounding West Berlin, of control over supply routes to it, and of the latent threat of numerically superior ground forces. The Allies and, after 1949, the Federal Republic had superior economic, legal, and moral resources to defend West Berlin against the threat of being absorbed into the GDR or turned into an "international" city under UN (not Allied) supervision. Keeping Berlin a part of the West was not only of interest to the two million West Berliners; symbolically it was also important for the future of a united Germany with its restored capital.

West Berlin's future thus depended on the solidarity between occupier and occupied. This close cooperation colored much of the city's postwar history, from the gratitude engendered by the Allied airlift during the Soviet blockade of 1948–49 to the enthusiasm of ordinary Berliners for John F. Kennedy, when the U.S. president declared himself to be one of them (*"Ich bin ein Berliner!"*). Allied and especially American aid to West Berlin took many forms, including founding a new university (the Free University) to replace the venerable but now Communist-dominated one in East Berlin. The fact that many Berliners moved to that half of the city that most corresponded to their ideological bent also reinforced particularly strong anticommunist and pro-American sentiments in West Berlin.

By the same token, West Berlin needed constant economic support from the West, notably from the Federal Republic. Cut off from its hinterland and laboring under the relative insecurity of its status, West Berlin could not compete on an equal footing with other commercial and industrial cities of West Germany. To offset the possibility (however remote) of a Soviet-backed takeover, the Bonn government sought to calm fears among capitalists by offering tax incentives for investment in West Berlin, for example. Massive public works projects kept money and employment pouring into the city. West Berlin was, among other things, to act as a showplace for Western capitalism and democracy.

This subsidization of West Berlin had many consequences, not all of which are of interest here. The artificial stimulation of the economy meant that work was plentiful (a fact that brought many foreign, especially Turkish, "guest workers" to the city), but housing was fairly cheap. Lavish subsidies for cultural activities meant that West Berlin's budget for the arts in the late 1980s was only half that of the entire American Endowment for the Arts. Under these circumstances, artists of all kinds found it easier to live and work in Berlin than in most other German cities.

These measures were also designed to combat the reluctance of young people to move to Berlin. The city had a disproportionate population of elderly people. Another peculiarity of West Berlin's status unintentionally supplied a large number of young people, however. When the Federal Republic was encouraged to rearm and join NATO in the mid-1950s, all able-bodied young men were subjected to the draft—unless they lived in Allied-administered West Berlin. This peculiar de-facto draft-exemption made the city attractive to pacifists and leftist critics of German rearmament, of NATO membership, and, in the late 1960s and early 1970s, of America's role in the Vietnam war.

The student "revolt" of the late 1960s was particularly pronounced in Berlin also. The Technical University in Charlottenburg and the Free University in the suburb of Dahlem were two of the biggest and best institutions of higher learning in Germany, lavishly subsidized and tuition-free. They drew tens of thousands of students from all over West Germany, many of whom (as in other metropolitan universities in Europe and America) regarded the universities as cells for social transformation more than as places to absorb traditional cultural values. The Free University (FU) especially was the scene of increasingly bitter student attacks on what they regarded as an authoritarian and undemocratic educational system from about 1965 on. Protests against America's Vietnam war added fuel to this movement of young people, and the cultural revolution of "hippies" against the traditional bourgeois lifestyle was at least as vocal in Berlin as in Berkeley. Demonstrations yielded street battles with police and martyrs such as Benno Ohnesorg and even the student leader Rudi Dutschke. The youth subculture paradoxically denounced capitalist, bourgeois society (especially in its American variant) while it embraced much of the pop culture from across the Atlantic.

Significantly, out of this revolt grew a permanent counterculture, generally dubbed *Die Szene* ("the Scene"), embracing many further subdivisions of great variety but vaguely united in opposition to the traditional capitalist "system," traditional political parties and middle-class life-styles. Ranging from gay-rights groups to opponents of nuclear power, to groups of "house-occupiers" who squatted in empty apartment buildings allegedly being kept off the market to boost rents in the city, this large urban counterculture endorsed alternatives to traditional concepts of life, work, and even art. (Indeed, Berlin's version of the West German Green Movement was called The Alternative List.)

Given the somewhat artificial structure of West Berlin's political system and economy, its geographical quarantine, its "showcase" function vis-à-vis surrounding East Germany, the large number of elderly and vocally anticommunist citizens, as well as the large and equally vocal critical counterculture spawned in the late 1960s, one could hardly expect the city to be dull culturally.

## CULTURAL CONTEXTS OF WALL ART

Berlin had its own cultural and artistic traditions from the pre-Nazi era. German expressionists, dadaists, members of the Bauhaus, and most other innovative cultural movements of the early twentieth century had left deep imprints on Berlin. It had also been the capital of popular culture in pre-1945 Germany, with its movie studios, cabarets, and "Broadway" music halls. The city had been a battleground, too, of strong political factions—Communists and Socialists, then Nazis—who promoted street demonstrations, banners, sloganeering, agitprop, marching songs, and every conceivable kind of means to mobilize the masses. One very apparent residue could until recently be seen anytime across the Wall in East Berlin. The omnipresent slogans and exhortations, in large white letters on red backgrounds, along with officially sanctioned "Socialist Realism" in the arts, almost cried out for mockery as they became increasingly stale reminders of the dead hand of Stalin.

The habit of writing on walls and buildings in the West was of course not government-sanctioned, which was precisely why the counterculture began doing it from the 1960s on. From Berkeley to Berlin, campus buildings became billboards of political programs, as well as of sometimes obscure and personal comments. As the movement to occupy vacant buildings and defend the squatters' rights against the authorities spread, so did the habit of covering the entire building with slogans and protest art.

If these local and ever-changing contexts for Wall art were not enough, West Berlin also imported a large and steady flow of visitors from West Germany and abroad. Tourists were not only encouraged to visit Berlin; such a trip was made out to be a patriotic act of solidarity for Germans and a Cold War duty for all citizens of the "Western world." Trains and buses disgorged their daily quota of schoolchildren, college students, and adults drawn to Berlin by the lure of cheap, subsidized travel to what few would deny was the most interesting city in Germany. A certain feeling that Berlin was a permissive city, and not only a beacon of Western freedom lighting up the surrounding terrain of Stalinist oppression, undoubtedly encouraged many tourists to do things there they would not have done in Rhöndorf or Dubuque, including writing on walls. Indeed, some experts on the history of the Wall maintain that most of the art on it must have been placed there by foreigners, given the heavy use of other languages, but this argument overlooks the bi- and even trilingualism of many Germans and most Berliners, or the dominance of English in the world youth subculture.

Berlin has always been the most cosmopolitan German city, at least since the turn of this century, and the loss of its political and economic centrality after 1945 paradoxically made it even more cosmopolitan. The competing ideas of East and West floated out on a vast tide of radio and TV broadcasts from both sides of the Wall, enabling the casual viewer to switch from *Dallas* to the All-Bulgarian Folk Dance Marathon and other improbable cultural contrasts available in no other city. In addition to the German-language programs, the Western Allies maintained their own radio and in some cases even TV networks in West Berlin. GIs, *poilus*, and Tommies mixed with the local population (introducing such cultural transfers as the American comic book). These influences were added to the already legendary Berlin flair for irreverence, biting wit, and satire. (Even East Berlin had officially to support one cabaret—*Die Distel*—where, and only where, it was permissible to laugh at the regime).

One can see from these background cultural elements an almost tailor-made opportunity for the emergence of graffiti as a new art form that was as much indigenous as borrowed from abroad. Added to that was the unique opportunity to deface public (GDR) property, simultaneously assailing "authority" and denying legitimacy to it, all while being cheered on by one's own fellow citizens (West). Given the slight possibility of unpleasantness from GDR border guards, writing on the Wall was a dangerous thrill, usually carried out under cover of darkness and therefore even more anonymous. Historians of Wall art appear to concur that graffiti were at first of the standard Kilroy and John-loves-Jane variety (and that this type probably constituted the majority of Wall dabblings to the end). But protests against the Wall and other political slogans, even punch lines of popular jokes at the expense of the GDR, expanded and enriched the repertory. Increasingly, too, cartoon-like representations as well as wordless imagery were added. Professional artists, known and unknown, added their bits, and the New York subway graffitist Keith Haring was even brought over to make a contribution.

What made Wall art especially interesting (and worth many revisits) was its emphemerality. Although GDR personnel would occasionally whitewash out sections of Wall art (especially if they found it outrageously offensive), they also realized that they were merely giving fresh "canvas" to the Wall artists. The more important factor lay in competition for prime center-city Wall space: other artists covered over the old images, even those by highly publicized international painters. Thus many images on the Wall are superimpositions and juxtapositions, transforming the original intent or message.

Much of the text on the Wall was all but indecipherable to the viewer, with its mixture of personal names and messages, obscene words, punch lines (or inversions) of jokes, political slogans, peace and environmental symbols, snatches of popular songs, quotations from literature or philosophy, insults and slurs, as well as counterculture catchphrases and intentionally obscure references, all in several languages. Leland Rice has consciously steered away from photographing these texts as such, preferring to focus on images or sections of images.

This is an understandable and perhaps necessary method of riveting the viewer's attention on the imagery, rather than the distracting ambiguity of the text. Even about a relatively clear and non-overlaid segment, such as *Hunger Herr Pastor* (Plate 9), one could write pages speculating on the references. One is to a novel *Der Hungerpastor* (1864) by the novelist Wilhelm Raabe, the "German Dickens," which one could translate as "the starving curate." Most German high-school students would at least be familiar with the title of this famous realist novel. But this three-word text is in the form of an admonition, "Hunger, Mr. Pastor," which could be in turn a leftist criticism of the inadequate provision for the starving of the world by organized Christianity (in turn affiliated with the conservative Christian Democratic party) or even a reference to the frequent appeals by precisely those churches to "give bread for the world." The burning skeleton and the vaguely Hitlerian face

d

to its left could be a reference to the Holocaust and its updated version (starvation). Yet the image would be just as compelling without the text.

Another image illustrated here, *Détente* (Plate 11), shows how clever and ambiguous textless images on the Wall could be. It shows a terrified Humpty Dumpty just clearing the wall in a leap to the observer's (Western) side, and still in mid-flight, apprehensive about Vopo bullets behind him, but probably unconscious of his fate (as we cannot be) when he hits the West Berlin pavement. Is this a restatement of the proverb about the grass being greener? Or resignation about the inability of all the king's horsemen (politicians?) being unable to put the (divided? polluted?) world back together again?

## THE END OF THE WALL

Ironically, the challenge of putting Berlin, Germany, and Europe back together again came with a suddenness that surprised everybody. Although political rhetoric in the West ritually called for an

Figure d. *East German watchtower near Checkpoint Charlie, 1985.*

end to the Wall, real expectations were that it would remain indefinitely. The hope was to humanize the GDR (exemplified in persuading the latter to stop shooting people who tried to escape), not to destroy the mighty Soviet empire and its German component. Much as Wall artists had to expect their works to have a short life, thanks to overpainting, few of them dreamed that they would swiftly fall prey to the hammers and chisels of the *Mauerspechte*, "woodpecking" the stone to crumbs as if it were rotten bark.

Erich Honecker, the East German leader, confidently said in January 1989 that he expected the Wall to last another fifty or one hundred years. He prepared for elaborate celebrations of the fortieth anniversary of the GDR in October 1989, with Gorbachev the guest of honor. The SED party leadership arrogantly said that the GDR did not need to embark on a Gorbachev-style *perestroika*, because it was already a model society. The East Germans, however, could barely afford to distance themselves from rigid Stalinism. Unlike other Soviet-bloc countries, such as Poland or Hungary, East Germany could not justify its existence in terms of nationalism. Masses of Poles would not flee their country (where would they go?) if they were given the chance, but would presumably stay to build a better society in a "reform" environment. But the GDR was either a communist-dominated country or none at all. Despite its propaganda efforts, the regime could convince nobody that it created a new kind of German national identity, distinct and separate from "capitalist national chauvinism" of the Western variety.

The chronology of crisis for the SED regime was brief. By 1989, the reform-minded Communist regime of Hungary made a gesture to its neighbor, Austria, in tearing down the barbed-wire barriers on their common borders. A few East German tourists (Hungary was one of the few places they were allowed to vacation) used the ceremony to flee to Austria. Soon Hungary was flooded with East Germans hoping to do the same—circumvent the Wall. After tense negotiations, Hungary let the East Germans go where they wanted, rather than forcing them to return to the GDR. Czechoslovakia, another Stalinist hard-line regime, then had the same problem, with the same outcome as in Hungary. Perhaps the SED reasoned that a couple hundred thousand opponents more or less would not hurt the regime, or that the touted fortieth anniversary must come off smoothly. But the absent workers, doctors, teachers (most of the refugees were young and highly qualified) already made a dent on the GDR's limping economy. Internally, as later became obvious, younger members of the SED leadership were also advocating the need for reforms.

Gorbachev seemed to support them, and not Honecker, at the anniversary celebrations, when he bluntly warned, "He who comes too late is punished by life." The growing weekly street demonstrations for reform, involving hundreds of thousands in cities like Leipzig, reminded the regime of the last challenge to it from the "gutter," in 1953. Then, Soviet tanks put down the East German uprising. Now, Gorbachev had made clear, Soviet intervention could not be expected. Honecker resigned; his hand-picked successor Egon Krenz had to promise change but lasted only a few weeks. One of these changes, however, announced almost off-handedly by a GDR functionary in November 1989 was the opening of the Wall. The GDR guards stood idly by, even smilingly accepted flowers, as Berliners climbed on the once-formidable barrier and celebrated the end of their division on November 9, 1989. The souvenir hunters quickly went to work on Wall art, for it was especially the painted parts of the structure that interested them. A few months later, most Wall art (and no doubt several hundred tons of other colored concrete) had wound up in thousands of living rooms from Berlin to Tokyo and Albuquerque, a mosaic diaspora unheard of in the history of art.

The breaching of the Wall was followed swiftly by the collapse of the GDR as a separate state and the overwhelming pressure from Germans East and West for immediate reunification. The end of the Wall (and after the GDR elections of March 1990, the last remnant of the SED regime) meant that Germans must become unified or face a gigantic migration from the GDR to the West, where they had a right to be cared for at public expense. After breathtakingly swift work by the two German governments and the four wartime Allies, and only days before the GDR would have celebrated its forty-first anniversary, Germany became a united and sovereign country again on October 3, 1990.

Just as revelations about the real workings of the GDR have outdone some of the worst charges of it enemies, inevitably in coming years some of the achievements of "real existing socialism" may be discussed dispassionately again, and a minority there, as in other Soviet bloc countries, persists in attempting to rescue salvageable parts from the Communist legacy. Yet no other bloc regime had to resort to such a drastic and symbolically visible measure as the Berlin Wall to keep its own people in. In drawing even more attention to it, by taking away some of its intimidating coldness with art, jokes, and human graffiti, the Wall artists probably also contributed to its end. Certainly unlike artists in most other times and places, it was a shared goal that their works *should* disappear as soon as possible.

It is nevertheless fitting that some of their imagery should be saved in this work by Leland Rice. Unlike most of the stale and lifeless imagery promoted as the official art of the German Democratic Republic, Berlin Wall art vibrates with the boundlessness of human creative urges and the need to express them freely.

*—Charles E. McClelland*

# PLATES

1.  *Aspects of a Nocturnal Passage, 1985*

2&3.  *(overleaf) Dark City (diptych), 1986*

4.  *Chaplin Mauer, 1985*

5.  *Ghetto Love, 1987*

6. *Burg, 1987*

7.  *Berlin Tex, 1985*

*8.  Exit, 1986*

Have you ever
en a antifashism
otection wall?
All that I
want to
know is which side
the fashist are on so
that I ca
be on the other side!
GEWON
DRAGON + KATH1

9. *Hunger Herr Pastor, 1986*

10.  *Walls of Perception, 1984*

11.  *Détente, 1985*

12.  *(overleaf) Lava (detail), 1987*

*13.  Volke, 1984*

*14.  Forever Friends, 1986*

15.  *Arbeiter und Bauren, 1985*

16.  *Yanks Out, 1985*

*17. Nous Nous, 1984*

*18. Tic Tac Geist, 1987*

*19. Fetting und die Mauer, 1986*

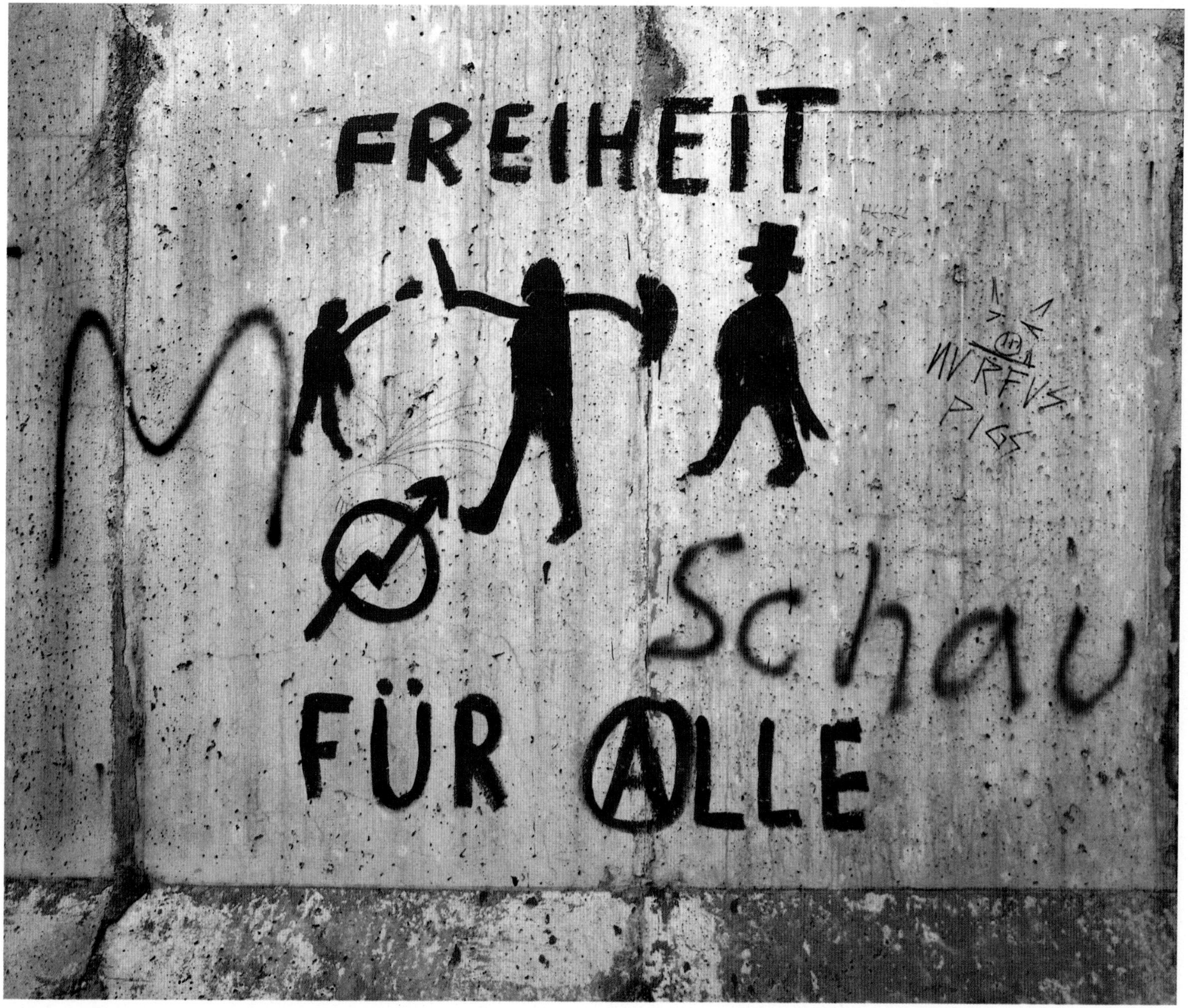
FREIHEIT
Schau
FÜR ALLE
NVRFVS
PIGS

22.  *So Look at Yourself Looking, 1987*

*23. Untitled (face), 1984*

*24. Wolfen, 1985*

*25.  Sex & Crime, 1984*

26. *Untitled (fish bowl), 1986*

27.  *Donald, 1987*

28.  *If They Can't Take Joke, 1985*

*29.  Bap, 1985*

*30. SAM, 1985*

*31. Low, 1986*

*32.  1984, 1985*

33.  *ESN, 1987*

34.  *(overleaf) Inka (detail), 1986*

*35. Tango King, 1987*

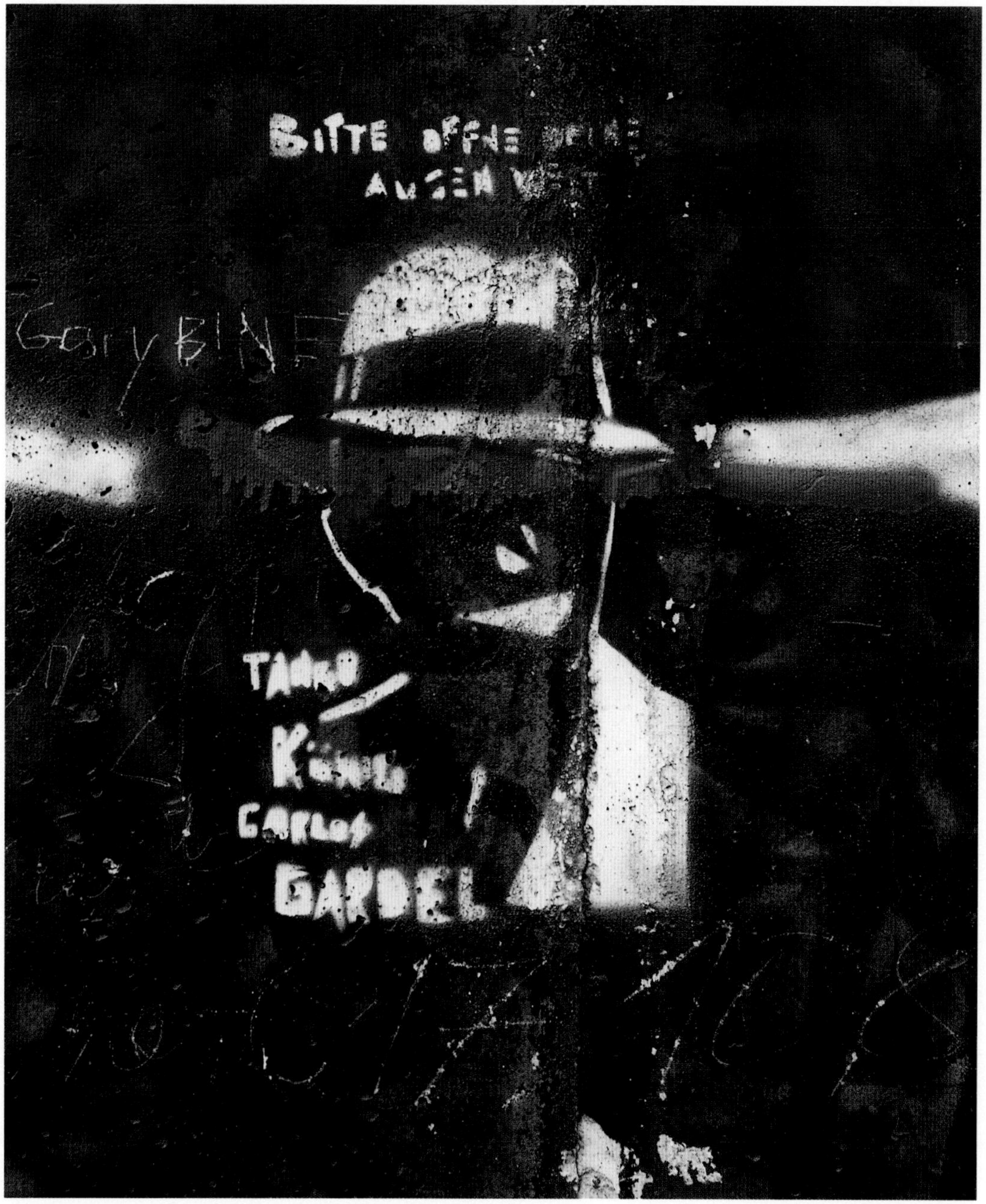
CARLOS
GARDEL

36.  *Runar, 1988*

37.  *Alleluia, 1983*

all abit confusing

ALLELUIA

BLA

POLS

Liebe Dörte,

weißt Du manchmal
habe ich einfach Angst
un Dich, weil ich Dich
liebe, Ich glaube nur Du
verstehst das.  R.

BRD

R  NAZ

Is this

*38. Indra, 1985*

# AFTERWORD

*"The wall gives its voice to that part of man which, without it, would
be condemned to silence . . . the remainder of a primitive existence of
which the wall may be one of the most faithful mirrors.
Graffiti is our state of civilization, our primitive art. . . ."*
—*Brassai,* The Language of the Wall:
Parisian Graffiti Photographed by Brassai
(*London: Institute of Contemporary Arts, 1958*)

MY FIRST ENCOUNTER WITH THE BERLIN WALL OCCURRED AT ABOUT
10,000 feet (in the air) in the fall of 1983 during a weekend adven-
ture that was hastily planned. Coming in by airplane to West Berlin,
I had three opportunities for aerial views of the Wall. At first the
brightly illuminated corridor along the Wall appeared to this night
traveler like a long snake encircling a large homogeneous settle-
ment. But by the third pass over the barrier I readjusted my quizz-
ical gaze to observe the buildings as massed like a group of captives
inside a fortress surrounded by threatening beams from the flood-

lights on the east side of the Wall. Upon landing, I concluded that such a dramatic introduction to this city only partially prepared me for the immense physical reality of its definitive border, the Wall.

Early the next morning I ventured out to take a walk along the Wall. While strolling along a well-traveled dirt path I began to observe the many spontaneous messages and markings scribbled on its flat pitted concrete surface. Accumulated over many years, countless graffiti had turned the Wall into a semantic playground full of forceful messages. I gradually realized that I no longer could relate to the Wall as just a physically tangible medieval barrier symbolizing the ideological division of Europe. Certainly the Wall did exist for divisive reasons, but now it took on another purpose for me—that of a creative catalyst. And, since walls had long been a primary subject of my work as an artist, I felt deeply compelled to photograph it.

Although the vast majority of the graffiti on the Wall was anonymous, we became the audience propelled into the same perspective as the unknown persons who provided the graffiti. We were also outside observers to the constantly changing imagery. The Wall was not a blackboard that gets erased regularly. Rather, the graffiti built to a crescendo of ever-elusive confusion. A rich pastiche of language and universal symbols coalesced to form a self-contained world. The essence of the writing on the Wall was best revealed by the energy that characterized the marks themselves. And, the essence of what I wanted to photograph was the profusion of images that spanned both popular culture derived from movies, television, and comic books, and abstracted figurative art forms.

The Wall also became a forum for wit and satire, and political sensibilities often were attacked through humorous graffiti on various levels of social critique. Most political messages I encountered were oversimplified metaphors playing upon an already awakened consciousness. They lacked visual profundity. However, the political significance of satire is pictorially evident in the image *Exit* (Plate 8), where spread across the back of partially clenched fingers are the words: "Have you ever seen an antifascism protection wall? All that I want to know is on which side the Fascists are on so that I can be on the other side." The incongruity between the text (the graffiti) and the context (the Wall) addresses the nature of this satirical and poignant communication. For the East German government, the Wall was a "protection" wall constructed to defend the socialist state from the imperialists of the capitalist West.

Now, some eight years later, and after five photographic pilgrimages since I began this project, the Wall has been dismantled. Graffiti has become an authentic signature of our urban centers. Drawing and inscribing on public walls are universal impulses in human nature. My approach to how I photographed the Wall was, in a broad sense, much like that of an archaeologist. I visually excavated fragments of layered subject matter to penetrate these "pentimento" surfaces and unearth the potential meanings of what I feel are contemporary pictographs reflecting our time.

*—Leland Rice*

# BIOGRAPHY OF THE ARTIST
## *Selected Bibliography*

For complete listing of exhibition catalogues and books published on the occasion of an exhibition, see individual exhibition listings.

This bibliography includes only works about the photography of Leland Rice and does not include Rice's catalogues, books, or articles on other photographers.

**Born**
Los Angeles, 1940

**Studied**
Arizona State University, Tempe, B.S., 1964; Chouinard Art Institute, Los Angeles, 1965; California State University, San Francisco (now San Francisco State University), M.A., 1969

**Taught**
California College of Arts and Crafts, Oakland, 1969–1972; University of California, Los Angeles, 1972, 1975, and 1982; California Institute of the Arts, Valencia, 1973; Pomona College, Claremont, California, 1973–1979; Tyler School of Art, Philadelphia, 1976; University of Southern California, Los Angeles, 1980–1981; University of Hartford, 1981

**Grants and Awards**
National Endowment for the Arts Photography Fellowship, 1978; John Simon Guggenheim Fellowship in Photography, 1979–80; James D. Phelan Art Award in Photography, 1986

## ONE-PERSON EXHIBITION CATALOGUES

**1977**

Millard, Charles W., ed. *The Photography of Leland Rice.* Washington, D.C.: Hirshhorn Museum and Sculpture Garden, Smithsonian Institution.

**1980**

*Leland Rice: Photography 1968–1980,* introduction by Richard Wickstrom. Las Cruces, New Mexico: University Art Gallery, New Mexico State University.

**1987**

*Leland Rice, Illusions and Allusions, Photographs of the Berlin Wall,* introduction by Van Deren Coke, afterword by Leland Rice. San Francisco: San Francisco Museum of Modern Art.

## SELECTED BOOKS AND EXHIBITION CATALOGUES WHICH INCLUDE THE ARTIST

**1969**

Lyons, Nathan. *Vision and Expression.* New York: Horizon Press and George Eastman House, Rochester, New York.

**1974**

Doty, Robert M. *Photography in America.* New York: Whitney Museum of American Art.

**1975**

Wise, Kelly, ed. *The Photographer's Choice.* Danbury, New Hampshire: Addison House.

**1976**

Mozley, Anita. *American Photography: Past Into Present, Prints from the Monsen Collection.* Seattle: Seattle Art Museum.

**1978**

"Enigmatic Portraits of Places," *Photography Year/1978.*
Alexandria, Virginia: Time-Life Books.

Szarkowski, John. *Mirrors and Windows: American
Photography since 1960.* New York: Museum of
Modern Art.

**1979**

Curran, Darryl. *Object Illusion Reality.* Fullerton,
California: Art Gallery, California State University,
Fullerton.

Witkin, Lee D., and Barbara London. *The Photograph
Collector's Guide.* Boston: New York Graphic Society.

**1980**

Glenn, Constance W., ed., with Jane K. Bledsoe. *Long
Beach: A Photographic Survey.* Long Beach,
California: Art Museum and Galleries, California
State University, Long Beach.

Van Dyke, Andrea. *Art in Our Time: The Collection of
the HHK Foundation for Contemporary Art,
Incorporated.* Milwaukee, Wisconsin: HHK
Foundation for Contemporary Art.

**1981**

Hunter, Sam. *New Directions: Contemporary American
Art from the Commodities Corporation Collection.* New
Jersey: Commodities Corporation.

**1982**

Johnson, Deborah J., ed. *California Photography.*
Providence: Museum of Art, Rhode Island School of
Design.

Walsh, George, Colin Naylor, and Michael Held, eds.
*Contemporary Photographers.* New York: Macmillan.

**1983**

Browne, Turner, and Elaine Partnow, eds. *Macmillan
Biographical Encyclopedia of Photographic Artists and
Innovators.* New York: Macmillan Publishing
Company.

Sweetman, Alex J. *Center of the Eye.* Colorado: Aspen
Center for the Visual Arts.

**1984**

Katzman, Louise. *Photography in California: 1945–1980.* San Francisco and New York: Hudson Hills Press, in associaton with San Francisco Museum of Modern Art.

Orr-Cahall, Christina, ed. *The Art of California: Selected Works from the Collection of The Oakland Museum.* Oakland and San Francisco: Oakland Museum Art Department and Chronicle Books.

**1987**

Grundberg, Andy, and Kathleen McCarthy Gauss. *Photography and Art: Interactions Since 1946.* New York: Abbeville Press.

Lemagny, Jean-Claude, and Andre Rouille. *A History of Photography.* Cambridge: Cambridge University Press.

McShine, Kynaston, ed. *BERLINART 1961–1987.* New York and Munich: Museum of Modern Art and Prestel Verlag.

**1988**

Ehrens, Susan. *The Consolidated Freightways, Inc. Collection.* Palo Alto, California: Consolidated Freightways, Inc.

**1990**

Valtorta, Roberta. *Writing on the Walls* [Scrieve sui muri]. Verona, Italy: World Action Project.

## SELECTED ARTICLES AND PORTFOLIOS

### 1969

"A Collection of Photographs from San Francisco State College," *San Francisco Camera* 1, no. 1 (January 1969).

"Photographs from California College of Arts and Crafts," *San Francisco Camera* 1, no. 3: 26, 27.

### 1970

Coleman, A. D. "California Report II: Those Who Can, Teach," *New York Times* (July 19): 19.

"A Selection of Photographs from the Pasadena Art Museum Permanent Collection, *San Francisco Camera* 1, no. 5.

"Visual Dialogue Foundation Members' Portfolio," *Album* 10, vol. 1, no. 2: 41.

### 1977

Heyman, Therese. "The Photography of Leland Rice," *Art* [a publication of the Art Guild of Oakland Museum Association] 5, no. 6 (November–December).

Lawrence, Sidney. "Rice Works in HMSG's [Hirshhorn Museum and Sculpture Garden] First Photo Exhibit," *Smithsonian Torch* (July): 2.

### 1978

Busch, Richard. "Leland Rice: Wall Sites," *Popular Photography* 83, no. 5 (November): 104–11, 188, 190.

Grundberg, Andy, and Julia Scully. "Currents: American Photography Today," *Modern Photography* (September): 82.

King, Pamela. "Leland Rice Turns the Commonplace into Art," *Los Angeles Herald-Examiner* (April 1): B3.

"Tyler in Color: 10th Anniversary of the Color Photography Program at Tyler School of Art," *Quiver*.

### 1979

Edwards, Owen. "The Eighties, Decade of Another Color," *Saturday Review* (May 12): 24–26, 31.

Hughes, Jim, ed. "Leland Rice: Wall Sites," *Color Annual 1979*. New York: Ziff-Davis, pp. 50–56, 109, 110.

Portner, Dinah. "An Interview with Leland Rice," *Journal: Southern California Art Magazine* 24 (September–October) [Los Angeles Institute of Contemporary Art]: 22–26.

Stevens, Nancy. "The Perils and Pleasures of Collecting Color," *Saturday Review* (May 12): 32–33.

**1980**

Grundberg, Andy, and Julia Scully. "Currents: American Photography Today," *Modern Photography* 44, no. 10 (October): 95.

**1983**

Johnson, Joyce Fay. "In Color: A Photographer's Choice," *The Museum of California* [The Oakland Museum] 6, no. 6 (May/June): 13–15.

**1985**

Muchnic, Suzanne. "Leland Rice Goes to the Wall—in Berlin," *Los Angeles Times* (May 12): Calendar, 73.

**1987**

Lufkin, Liz. "Messages from the Wall: Graffiti of the Berlin Wall Photographed by Leland Rice," *San Francisco Chronicle, THIS WORLD* (August 9): 10–12.

Skinner, Peter. "Leland Rice: Images of the Berlin Wall," *The World & I* 2, no. 11 (November): 242–45.

Smith, Linnell. "Berlin Wall Graffiti Mute but Eloquent," *Baltimore Sun* (October 3): C1, C7.

**1990**

Marable, Darwin. "Leland Rice's Photographs of the Berlin Wall Graffiti." In *Shadow and Substance: Essays on the History of Photography in Honor of Heinz K. Henisch*, Kathleen Collins, ed. Michigan: Amorphous Institute Press, 1990.

Sullivan, Meg. "Berlin Wall: Not Just Another Souvenir," *Daily News* (June 13): 9.

### SELECTED EXHIBITION REVIEWS

**1969**

Albright, Thomas. "A Spooky Expression," *San Francisco Chronicle* (June).

Bry, Michael E. "Gallery Snooping," *Modern Photography* (July): 24, 26.

**1970**

Albright, Thomas. "California Photographers," *San Francisco Chronicle* (June 6).

Coleman, A. D. "Latent Image," *Village Voice* (April 9): 20.

———. "Four San Francisco Photographers," *Village Voice* (April 9).

Mann, Margery. "View from the Bay," *Popular Photography* (August): 25, 26.

Thornton, Gene. "The Question Is, Does it 'Hold the Wall'?" *New York Times* (April 19).

Wilson, William. "Pasadena Shows Are Study in Poetic Exhaustion," *Los Angeles Times* (July 19).

**1971**

Coleman, A. D. "Four Photographs that Drove a Man to Crime," *New York Times* (April 11).

**1972**

Murray, Joan. "Ward and Rice in Carmel," *Artweek* (May 20): 9–10.

**1973**

Andre, Michael. "Reviews and Previews," *Artnews* (December): 89.

Coleman, A. D. "She Studies People, He Fantasizes," *New York Times* (November 4): sec. 2, 35.

**1974**

Mautner, Robert. "Photography 1974—Added Dimension," *Artweek* (February 16): 11–12.

Thornton, Gene. "From Artistic to Glamorous," *New York Times* (February 3): sec. 2, 32.

Wortz, Melinda. "Kasten and Rice," *Artweek* (March 23): 3.

**1975**

Fishman, Lois. "Following Relationships in Time," *Artweek* (May 31): 11–12.

**1976**

Eauclaire, Sally. "Photographers, Artists Borrow from Each Other," *Rochester Democrat and Chronicle* (October 7): 2C.

Wilson, William. "Photography Looking for Itself through the Lens," *Los Angeles Times* (November 7): Calendar, 72.

**1977**

Albright, Thomas. "Provocative Photographs of the 'Missing,'" *San Francisco Chronicle* (November 30): 51.

Fondiller, Harvey V. "Shows We've Seen," *Popular Photography* (November): 28.

Mautner, Robert. "Silver See, An Overview of Los Angeles Work," *Artweek* (September 24).

Murray, Joan. "The Visual Dialogue Foundation at Carmel," *Artweek* (February 19).

———. "Objects and Environments with Inner Life," *Artweek* (November 19): 9–10.

**1978**

Davis, Douglas. "Mirrors and Windows," *Newsweek* (August 14): 69–72.

Muchnic, Suzanne. "Symbiosis of Canvas and Camera," *Los Angeles Times* (April 1): sec. II, 11.

Wortz, Melinda. "Esthetics of Emptiness," *Artnews* (October): 139.

**1979**

Johnstone, Mark. "Leland Rice Walls," *Artweek* (June 2): 13.

Muchnic, Suzanne. "Photography as Art and History," *Los Angeles Times* (March 11).

———. "Art Walk: A Critical Guide to the Galleries," *Los Angeles Times* (May 25): Part IV, 18.

———. "Road Maps to Connections, Classicism," *Los Angeles Times* (May 27): Calendar, 81–82.

Noah, Barbara. "Leland Rice at Rosamund Felsen," *Art in America* 67, no. 7 (November): 131.

Wilson, William. "Photography—The State of the Art," *Los Angeles Times* (January 28): 87.

**1980**

Albright, Thomas. "A Pleasant Nostalgic Excursion," *San Francisco Chronicle* (February 15).

———. "A Touch of Surrealism," *San Francisco Chronicle* (March 24): 47.

Hedgpeth, Ted. "Meaning in Whispers," *Artweek* (March 29): 13.

Wigginton, Mark. "Long Beach Images: Art and Archives," *Independent Press-Telegram* (November 10): C9.

**1981**

Badger, Gerry. "California Colour," *Creative Camera* 202 (October): 246–47.

Johnstone, Mark. "Unfinished Business" [exhibition review: *Long Beach: A Photography Survey*], *Afterimage* 8, no. 7 (February): 13.

———. "Information Becomes a Vision," *Artweek* (June).

Muchnic, Suzanne. "A Spectrum of Colorists," *Los Angeles Times* (February 8): Calendar, 89.

Sturken, Marita. "Curatorial Quirks, and The Camera Arts," *Afterimage* (Summer): 6–7.

Wilson, William. "The Galleries," *Los Angeles Times* (April 24): Part VI.

**1982**

Thornton, Gene. "A Color Show Out of Focus," *New York Times* (April 25): D7.

Knight, Christopher. "Photos that Shun the 'Real World,'" *Los Angeles Herald Examiner* (August 1): E4.

Muchnic, Suzanne. "Photos That Are Made, Not Found," *Los Angeles Times* (September 1): 1, 4.

**1983**

Murray, Joan. "Color!!" *Artweek* (July 2): 11–12.

Shere, Charles. "Art Blends into Other Art," *Oakland Tribune Calendar* (June 12): 24.

Thompson, Barbara. "In Color: Ten California Photographers at the Oakland Museum," *Photo Metro* (July): 19.

**1984**

Albright, Thomas. "Study in Lopsidedness," *San Francisco Chronicle* (January 22): *Review,* 12–13.

———. "Photochic," *Artnews* (April): 73–78.

Asbury, Dana. "Show's We've Seen," *Popular Photography* (October): 33–34, 42, 44, 46.

Davis, Douglas. "California by Strobe Light," *Newsweek* (March 5): 80–81.

Muchnic, Suzanne. "Exploring Emotional Connections in 'Spirits,'" *Los Angeles Times* (September 16): 97.

Murray, Joan. "An Embarrassing Exhibition," *Artweek* (February 11): 11–12.

Starenko, Michael. "History and Geography: The California (Photography) Lesson," *Afterimage* 11, no. 10 (May): 12–17.

Stathatos, John. "Photography in California, 1945–1980," *Creative Camera* (October): 1554–59.

Wilson, William. "Report on a Medium in Crisis," *Los Angeles Times* (September 16): 97.

**1985**

Gardner, Colin. "Photography: Leland Rice—A Wall-to-Wall Witness," *L.A. Reader* (May 17): 6.

Nicholson, Chuck. "Art and Graffiti," *Artweek* (May 25): 11.

Wilson, William. "The Art Galleries," *Los Angeles Times* (May 17): 10.

**1986**

Muchnic, Suzanne. "Exploring Emotional Connections in 'Spirits,'" *Los Angeles Times* (May 5): Part VI, 1, 6.

Wilson, William. "The Art Galleries," *Los Angeles Times* (October 17): 19.

**1987**

Baker, Kenneth. "Up Against the Wall—Cool Views of Hot Subject," *San Francisco Chronicle* (August 22): 37.

Cotter, Holland. "Art from the Exiled City," *Art in America* (October): 43–49.

Dorsey, John. "Rice Captures Eloquence in Berlin Wall Graffiti," *Baltimore Sun* (October 6): 1–2C.

Durant, Mark. "Modern Photography and Ideology: Leland Rice at SFMMA," *Photo Metro* (October): 28–29.

Fowler, Carol. "Art from the Berlin Wall," *Contra Costa Times* (November 21): 8B.

Gadd, David. "Leland Rice's Photo at SFMMA: Writing on the Wall," *San Francisco Sentinel* (August 21): 23.

Hughes, Robert. "Out of the Wall's Shadow," *Time* (August 24): 64–65.

Knight, Christopher. "Putting 'Photography and Art' in Sharp Focus," *Los Angeles Herald Examiner* (June 14): E2.

Larson, Kay. "Divide and Conquer," *New York* (June 22): 74–75.

Marable, Darwin. "Watching the Wall," *Artweek* (September 26): 6–7.

McColm, Del. "Graffiti: It's War on the Streets, It's Art in Museum," *The Davis Enterprise Weekend* (September 23): 7.

Wilson, William. "Up-to-Date Berlin Art: Link to L.A.," *Los Angeles Times* (June 28): Calendar, 106, 108.

**1988**

Dorsey, John. "Berlin Wall Photos Making Reference to Art as well as Politics," *Baltimore Sun* (December 1): 1G, 8G.

**1990**

Jarrell, Joe. "Berlin Wall Exhibit: Pieces of a Dream," *Village View* [Los Angeles] (June 22–28).

Jennings, Kate F. "Berlin Wall Reveals Lively Art," *Greenwich* [Ct.] *News* (April 12): A40.

**Unpublished Source**

*Interview with Leland Rice*, California Oral History Project, Archives of American Art, Smithsonian Institution. Interview conducted by Louise Katzman, San Francisco Museum of Modern Art, June 18, 1981. Transcript, 83 pages.

# Selected Exhibition History

## SELECTED ONE-PERSON EXHIBITIONS

### 1972
Déjà Vu Gallery, Los Angeles

Friends of Photography Gallery, Carmel, California, April 29–June 4.

Center of the Eye, "Smoke" Gallery, Aspen, Colorado, June.

### 1973
Witkin Gallery, New York, October 23–December 2.

### 1974
School of the Art Institute of Chicago, Illinois.

### 1975
California State University, Northridge.

*Wall Sites*, Diablo Valley College Art Gallery, Pleasant Hills, California, January 10–February 7.

### 1976
*Leland Rice, Wall Sites*, Jack Glenn Gallery, Newport Beach, California, January 10–February 6.

Visual Studies Workshop, Rochester, New York, September 10–October 15.

### 1977
*The Photography of Leland Rice*, Hirshhorn Museum and Sculpture Garden, Smithsonian Institution, Washington, D.C., June 16–September 5. Traveled to Oakland Museum, California, October 25–January 7, 1978. Catalogue.

*Leland Rice, Color Photographs*, Diane Brown Gallery, Washington, D.C., June 16–July 16.

*Leland Rice: New Color Photographs*, Witkin Gallery, New York, July 20–August 20.

**1978**

*The Photography of Leland Rice*, University Art Gallery, University of Southern California, Los Angeles, March 9–April 13.

*Leland Rice: New Color Works*, Photography Gallery, Orange Coast College, Costa Mesa, California, November 13–December 1.

**1979**

*Recent Color Photographs*, Rosamund Felsen Gallery, Los Angeles, May 15–June 8.

Diane Brown Gallery, Washington, D.C., June 2–23.

**1980**

*Leland Rice: Color Photographs*, Grapestake Gallery, San Francisco, March 13–April 19.

*Leland Rice: Photographs 1968–1980*, University Art Gallery, New Mexico State University, Las Cruces, October 1–November 5. Catalogue.

**1981**

*New Color Photographs*, Rosamund Felsen Gallery, Los Angeles, April 18–May 16.

**1985**

*Die Mauer: Cibachrome Photographs of the Berlin Wall*, Rosamund Felsen Gallery, Los Angeles, May 4–June 1.

**1986**

*Recent Photographs of the Berlin Wall*, Rosamund Felsen Gallery, Los Angeles, October 11–November 8.

**1987**

*Leland Rice: Illusions and Allusions, Photographs of the Berlin Wall*, San Francisco Museum of Modern Art, August 13–November 1. Catalogue

*Leland Rice: Photographs of the Berlin Wall*, Baltimore Museum of Art, Maryland, October 6–November 29.

**1988**

*Leland Rice: Photographs of the Berlin Wall*, Kouros Gallery, New York, November 17–December 31. Brochure.

*Leland Rice: Wall Photographs 1978–1988*, C. Grimaldis Gallery, Baltimore, Maryland, December 1–31. Brochure.

**1989**

Leland Rice: *Photographs of the Berlin Wall*, Santa
Monica College, September 22–November 9.

**1990**

*Leland Rice: Berlin Wall Photographs*, C. Grimaldis
Gallery, Baltimore, Maryland, January 3–February
24.

*Leland Rice: Graffiti from the Berlin Wall, A
Photographic Memory*, Kouros Gallery, New York,
January 13–February 17.

*Graffiti from the Berlin Wall by Leland Rice*, Barney's
Art Gallery, Greenwich, Connecticut, March 23–April
20.

*The Berlin Wall*, Tennessee Avenue Art Space, Los
Angeles, June 12–July 4.

**1991**

*Leland Rice Wall Sites* [two one-person exhibitions:
Leland Rice and Burgoyne Diller], Harcourt Modern
and Contemporary Art, San Francisco, January 10–
February 9.

## SELECTED GROUP EXHIBITIONS

**1968**

*Young Photographers*, University Art Museum,
University of New Mexico, Albuquerque. Traveled to
Mills College Art Gallery, Oakland, California;
Madison Art Center, Wisconsin; Columbia Museum
of Art, Columbia, South Carolina; University Gallery,
University of Florida, Gainesville. Catalogue.

*Young Photographers '68*, Purdue University Art
Museum, Purdue, Indiana, April 1–30. Traveling
exhibition. Catalogue.

*Rolling Renaissance Photography: The Scene and
Portraits 1945–1968*, Light Sound Dimension Gallery,
San Francisco, June 5–20. Catalogue.

**1969**

*Vision and Expression*, George Eastman House,
Rochester, New York, Feburary 28–May 11. Traveled
to St. Thomas University Media Center, Champaign,
Illinois; Amon Carter Museum, Fort Worth; El Paso
Museum of Art; Sheridan College, Brampton,

Ontario; University of Connecticut at Storrs; Illinois State University, Normal; San Francisco Museum of Art. Book published on the occasion of the exhibition.

*Visual Dialogue Foundation,* Center of the Visual Arts, Oakland, California, March 25–April 25. Catalogue.

*Photographs: Michael Bishop, Judy Dater, Clyde H. Dilly, Leland Rice, John Spence Weir,* San Francisco Museum of Art, July 3–27. Brochure.

*Recent Acquisitions 1969,* Pasadena Art Museum, California, November 24–January 18, 1970. Catalogue.

## 1970

*Visual Dialogue Foundation Founders' Portfolio,* Focus Gallery, San Francisco, March 31–April 25.

*New Realism: Four San Francisco Photographers: Leland Rice, Judy Dater, John Spence Weir, Jack Welpott,* Witkin Gallery, New York, April 1–May 3.

*California Photographers 1970,* Memorial Union Art Gallery, University of California, Davis, April 6–May

9. Traveled to Oakland Museum, California; Pasadena Art Museum, California. Catalogue.

*The Metropolitan Middle Class,* Creative Photography Gallery, Massachusetts Institute of Technology, Cambridge, April 10–May 1.

## 1971

*Photography Invitational 1971,* Arkansas Art Center, Little Rock, January 14–February 11. Traveled to Memphis Academy of Arts, Tennessee; Minneapolis Institute of Art. Catalogue.

*Centennial Exhibition,* San Francisco Art Institute, January 15–February 28. Catalogue.

*A Variety Show,* Art Gallery, Humboldt State University, Arcata, California, April 5–23.

*Young California Photographers,* Musée Reattu, Arles, France, June 16–July 14.

*The Visual Dialogue Foundation,* Image Works Gallery, Boston.

**1972**

*The Visual Dialogue Foundation*, Friends of
Photography, Carmel, California, February 4–March
10. Traveled to Pasadena Art Museum (in altered
form). Catalogue.

*Recent Acquisitions*, Galerie de Photographie de la
Bibliothèque Nationale, Paris.

*Survey of Southern California Photography*, Los Angeles
County Museum of Art.

*Critics' Choice* (curated by Thomas Albright), Focus
Gallery, San Francisco, October 10–November 4.

**1973**

*Photographs from the Permanent Collection*, Pasadena
Art Museum, June 5–July 29.

*The Document*, Tyler School of Art, Philadelphia.

*Collectors' Choice II*, Focus Gallery, San Francisco,
December 4–January 5, 1974.

**1974**

*Language of Light*, University of Kansas Museum of
Art, Lawrence, February 3–24. Catalogue.

*Photography 1974—Added Dimension*, Los Angeles
County Museum of Art Rental Gallery.

*Leland Rice and Barbara Kasten*, Ross-Freeman Gallery,
Northridge, California, March 1–30.

*Photography West*. Utah State University, Logan, Utah.

*Photography in America*, Whitney Museum of American
Art, New York, November 20–January 12, 1975.
Book published on the occasion of the exhibition.

**1975**

*History Transformed, History of Photography as Subject
Matter*, Orange Coast College Art Gallery, Costa
Mesa, California, February 25–March 21. Traveled to
Friends of Photography, Carmel, California.

*First Light*, Art Gallery, Humboldt State University,
Arcata, California, March 29–April 14. Traveled to
Focus Gallery, San Francisco.

*Recent Works by Ten Photographers*, Frederick S. Wight
Gallery, University of California, Los Angeles, July
15–August 15.

**1976**

*Photographers' Choice*, Mount St. Mary's College Art Gallery, Los Angeles, February 9–March 21. Traveled to Witkin Gallery, New York; Colby-Sawyer College, New London, New Hampshire; Enjay Gallery, Boston; University of Tennessee, Knoxville; Dartmouth College, Hanover, New Hampshire; Apeiron Workshop, Millerton, New York; University of Florida, Gainesville; Adams State College, Alamosa, Colorado; Millikin University, Decatur, Illinois; Art Institute of Pittsburgh; Southwest Missouri State University; Springfield; Arkansas Art Center, Little Rock. Book published on the occasion of the exhibition.

*American Photography: Past Into Present/Prints from the Monsen Collection of American Photography*, March 4–April 11. Traveled to Portland Art Museum, Portland, Oregon. Book published on the occasion of the exhibition.

*Twentieth Century Photographers in the Collection*, Galleries of the Claremont Colleges, Montgomery Art Gallery, Claremont, California, March–April.

*Exposing: Photographic Definitions*, Los Angeles Institute of Contemporary Art, October 26–December 3. Catalogue.

Visual Studies Workshop, Rochester, New York.

*First Photographic Invitational*, University of Nevada, Reno.

*Rooms*, Museum of Modern Art, New York.

**1977**

*The Light in the Interior*, Museum of Fine Arts, Boston, March 19–June 5.

*Photography into Painting*, Silver Image Gallery, Seattle, September 8–October 2.

*Contemporary Photography*, Indiana University Art Museum, Bloomington.

*A Photography Show*, Kress-Sonora Gallery, Taos, New Mexico.

*100+ Current Directions in Southern California Art*, Los Angeles Institute of Contemporary Art.

**1978**

*Forty American Photographers*, E. B. Crocker Art
  Gallery, Sacramento, California, February 4–March
  5. Catalogue.

*The Photograph as Artifice*, Art Galleries, California
  State University, Long Beach, April 3–30. Traveled
  to Grossmont College Art Gallery, El Cajon,
  California; Friends of Photography Gallery, Carmel,
  California; Santa Barbara Museum of Art,
  California; California State Polytechnic University,
  Pomona; Hyde Collection, Glen Falls, New York;
  Helen Foresman Spencer Museum, University of
  Kansas, Lawrence; Community Gallery of Lancaster
  County, Pennsylvania; Bruce Gallery, Edinboro State
  College, Pennsylvania. Catalogue.

*Photographs from the Permanent Collection*, San
  Francisco Museum of Modern Art, April 21–June 11.
  Catalogue.

*Mirrors and Windows: American Photography Since
  1960*, Museum of Modern Art, New York, July 28–
  October 2. Traveled to Cleveland Museum of Art,
  Ohio; Walker Art Center, Minneapolis; J. B. Speed

Art Museum, Louisville, Kentucky; San Francisco
  Museum of Modern Art; Krannert Art Museum,
  University of Illinois, Champaign; Virginia Museum
  of Fine Arts, Richmond; Milwaukee Art Center.
  Catalogue.

*Photography: Four Stylistic Approaches*, Katonah
  Gallery, Katonah, New York.

*Thanatopsis: Contemplations on Death*, Space Gallery,
  Los Angeles, September 12–October 21.

**1979**

*Photographic Directions: Los Angeles, 1979*, Security
  Pacific Bank, Los Angeles, January 9–February 26.
  Catalogue.

*Southern California Invitational '79 Photography Survey*,
  University Art Galleries, University of Southern
  California, Los Angeles, February 9–April 27.

*Attitudes: Photography in the 1970s*, Santa Barbara
  Museum of Art, May 12–August 5. Catalogue.

*Eleven from "Mirrors and Windows,"* Grapestake
  Gallery, San Francisco, June 7–July 28.

*Four California Photographers*, Light Gallery, New York,
  July 10–31.

*Object/Illusion/Reality*, Art Gallery, California State
    University, Fullerton, September 21–October 18.
    Catalogue.

*Tyler in Color*, Tyler School of Art Gallery, Philadelphia,
    October 11–28.

*Black + White + Color*, Creative Photography Gallery,
    Massachusetts Institute of Technology, Cambridge,
    October 23–November 29.

*Spectrum: New Directions in Color Photography*,
    University of Hawaii, Manoa, November 17–
    December 16. Traveled to University of Hawaii,
    Hilo; Hui Noeau, Maui; Garden Isle Arts Council,
    Kauai; Washington State University, Pullman; Tyler
    Museum of Art, Tyler, Texas; Virginia Beach Art
    Center, Virginia; Galleries of the Claremont Colleges,
    Claremont, California; Georgia Museum of Art,
    Athens; Northwest Community College, Powell,
    Wyoming; University of North Colorado, Greeley.
    Catalogue.

**1980**

*Photographic Scale*, Art Gallery, Sonoma State
    University, Rohnert Park, California, January 30–
    February 22.

*Bay Area Photographers 1954–1979*, Focus Gallery, San
    Francisco, February 5–March 1.

*Aspects of the 70s, Photography: Recent Directions*,
    DeCordova Museum, Lincoln, Massachusetts, June
    1–August 31. Catalogue.

*Art in Our Time: The Collection of the HHK Foundation
    for Contemporary Art, Incorporated*, Milwaukee Art
    Center, October 9–November 30. Traveled to
    Contemporary Art Center, Cincinnati, Ohio;
    Columbus Museum of Art, Ohio; Virginia Museum of
    Fine Arts, Richmond; Krannert Art Museum,
    University of Illinois, Champaign; High Museum of
    Art, Atlanta; University of Iowa Museum of Art, Iowa
    City; Brooks Memorial Art Gallery, Memphis,
    Tennessee; University Art Museum, Austin, Texas.
    Catalogue.

*Recent Color Photographs by David Haxton, Leland Rice, and Sandy Skoglund,* CEPA Gallery, Buffalo, New York, October 18–November 24.

*Long Beach: A Photographic Survey,* Art Museum and Galleries, California State University, Long Beach, November 10–December 14. Catalogue.

*New Work,* Rosamund Felsen Gallery, Los Angeles, December 8–January 3, 1981.

**1981**

*The Whitney 1981 Biennial,* Whitney Museum of American Art, New York, January 20–April 5. Catalogue.

*Object, Illusion, Reality,* United States International Communication Agency, Washington, D.C. Traveled to Belgrade Museum of Modern Art, Yugoslavia; Van Reekum Museum of Modern Art, The Hague; Palais des Beaux Arts, Brussels, Belgium; North Outland Museum of Art, Aslborg, Denmark.

*A Look at the Boundaries: 14 California Photographers,* Memorial Union Art Gallery, University of California, Davis, March 23–April 24. Brochure.

*California Colour,* Photographers' Gallery, London, England, July 15–September 13. Catalogue.

*Facets of the Collection: Color and Colored Photographs 1938–1979,* San Francisco Museum of Modern Art, October 2–November 15.

*Locations,* Art Gallery, California State College, San Bernadino, October 9–November 4. Catalogue.

*Leland Rice, Linda Conner, Barbara Blondeau,* Looking Glass Gallery, Royal Oak, Michigan, October 16–November 20.

*New Directions: Contemporary American Art from the Commodities Corporation Collection.* Traveled to Museum of Art, Fort Lauderdale, Florida; Oklahoma Museum of Art, Oklahoma City; Santa Barbara Museum of Art, California; Grand Rapids Art Museum, Michigan; Madison Art Center, Wisconsin; Montgomery Museum of Fine Arts, Alabama. Catalogue.

**1982**

*California Photographers,* Museum of Art, Rhode Island School of Design, Providence, January 8–February 7. Catalogue.

*Color as Form: A History of Color Photography*, Corcoran Gallery of Art, Washington, D.C., April 9–June 6. Traveled to International Museum of Photography at George Eastman House, Rochester, July 2–September 6. Catalogue.

*Studio Work: Photographs by Ten Los Angeles Artists*, Los Angeles County Museum of Art, July 22–October 31. Catalogue.

**1983**

*California College of Arts and Crafts: 75 Years*, San Francisco Museum of Modern Art, January 18–February 27. Catalogue.

*In Color: Ten California Photographers*, Oakland Museum, Oakland, California, May 21–July 17. Brochure.

**1984**

*Leland Rice and Gloria DeFilipps Brush: Colors, Shapes and Spaces*, Film in the Cities, Minneapolis, January 10–31.

*Ten California Photographers*, Grapestake Gallery, San Francisco, January 26–March 3.

*Landscapes, Figures, Objects: The Implied Performance*, Contemporary Photographs from the Permanent Collection of the San Francisco Museum of Modern Art, Art Gallery, California State University, Northridge, March 5–30.

*Color in the Summer*, Brooklyn Museum, New York, July 19–September 30.

*Photography in California: 1945–1980*, San Francisco Museum of Modern Art, San Francisco, January 12–March 11. Traveled to Akron Art Museum, Ohio; Corcoran Art Gallery, Washington, D.C.; Los Angeles Municipal Art Gallery, Barnsdall Park; Herbert F. Johnson Museum of Art, Cornell University, Ithaca; High Museum of Art, Atlanta, Georgia; Museum Folkwang, Essen, West Germany; Musée National d'Art Modern, Centre Georges Pompidou, Paris; Museum of Photographic Arts, San Diego, California. Book published on the occasion of the exhibition.

**1985**

*Imagine There's a Future*, USC Atelier, Santa Monica, California, July 20–September 1.

*Contemporary West Coast Color Photography*, Crocker Art Museum, Sacramento, California, August 10–October 20. Brochure.

*Progressive Collecting*, Photography Gallery, LaJolla, California, October 5–November 23.

**1986**

*The Exhibition Award Winners for the James D. Phelan Award in Photography*, San Francisco Camerawork Gallery, February 11–March 8.

*Kindred Spirits* [includes Leland Rice's Wall Site photographs with Larry Bell's sculpture], Los Angeles Municipal Art Gallery, Barnsdall Art Park, April 29–June 1. Catalogue.

**1987**

*Poignant Sources*, Artspace, San Francisco, March 10–April 18. Brochure.

*BERLINART 1961–1987*, Museum of Modern Art, New York, June 4–September 8. Traveled to San Francisco Museum of Modern Art. Book published on the occasion of the exhibition.

*Photography and Art: Interactions since 1946*, Los Angeles County Museum of Art, June 4–August 30. Traveled to Museum of Art, Fort Lauderdale, Florida; Queens Museum, Flushing, New York; Des Moines Art Center, Des Moines, Iowa. Book published on the occasion of the exhibition.

*Berlin von Aussen (Berlin from the Outside)*, Akademie der Kunste, Berlin, June 13–August 2.

*Hommage a Berlin*, Gerd Sander Gallery, New York, June 3–13.

*Chairs: A Show of Photographs and Sculpture*, Witkin Gallery, New York, July 14–August 21.

**1989**

*Art Against Aids, on the Road*, Butterfields and Butterfields, San Francisco, May 18–June 18. Catalogue.

*People, Places and the Environment*, Transamerica
Galleries, Los Angeles, July 8–September 4.
Brochure.

*Framing Four Decades*, University Art Museum,
California State University, Long Beach, August 25–
October 9. Catalogue.

*The Collector's Eye: New Mexico Collects*, Museum of
Fine Arts, Museum of New Mexico, Santa Fe,
December 16–April 22, 1990.

### 1990

*The Wall: An Installation of German and American
Artists*, Foster Goldstrom, New York, January 13–
February 16.

*Writing on the Walls [Scrieve sui muri]*, Casa di
Giulietta, Verona, Italy, organized by the World
Action Project, September 8–October 31. Book
published on the occasion of the exhibition.

## MUSEUM COLLECTIONS

Art Institute of Chicago

Baltimore Museum of Art

Bibliothèque Nationale, Paris

California State University, Long Beach

Center for Creative Photography, University of Arizona,
Tucson

Corcoran Gallery of Art, Washington, D.C.

Denver Art Museum

Fogg Art Museum, Harvard University

International Center of Photography, New York

International Museum of Photography at George
Eastman House, Rochester, New York

Los Angeles County Museum of Art

Metropolitan Museum of Art, New York

Minneapolis Institute of Art

Musée Cantini Art Contemporain, Marseille, France

Musée Reattu, Arles, France

Museum of Art, Rhode Island School of Design,
Providence

Museum of Fine Arts of St. Petersburg, Florida

Museum of Modern Art, New York

National Gallery of Canada, Ottawa

New Orleans Museum of Art

Newport Harbor Art Museum, California

Norton Simon Museum of Art, Pasadena, California

Oakland Museum, California

Phoenix College, Phoenix, Arizona

Pomona College, Claremont, California

Princeton University Art Museum

Saint Louis Art Museum

San Francisco Museum of Modern Art

Seattle Art Museum

University of California at Los Angeles

University of Colorado at Boulder

University of Kansas, Lawrence

University of New Mexico, Albuquerque

Vassar College, Poughkeepsie, New York

Visual Studies Workshop, Rochester, New York

**UP AGAINST IT**
DESIGNED BY KRISTINA E. KACHELE
IN CONSULTATION WITH LELAND RICE
COMPOSITION BY VANGIE MARES OF
THE UNIVERSITY OF NEW MEXICO PRINTING SERVICES
WITH PRODUCTION BY DON LEISTER
PRINTED BY DAI NIPPON PRINTING COMPANY, LTD., JAPAN